# Out *of the* Ashes

ALSO BY COURTNEY PEPPERNELL

*Pillow Thoughts*

*Pillow Thoughts: Deluxe Edition*

*Pillow Thoughts II: Healing the Heart*

*Pillow Thoughts III: Mending the Mind*

*Pillow Thoughts IV: Stitching the Soul*

*The Road Between*

*I Hope You Stay*

*The Space Between Us*

*Watering the Soul*

*The Way Back Home*

*Time Will Tell*

*A Month of Sundays*

# Out *of the* Ashes

Courtney Peppernell

Andrews McMeel
PUBLISHING®

# *Acknowledgments*

Like all the many other projects I have worked on, it is a team effort. I would like to thank everyone at Andrews McMeel, especially Liz, Danys, Patty, Diane, and Kirsty, for all your unwavering efforts. James, for all that you do behind the scenes, you are irreplaceable. Justin, my illustrator, who has wonderfully brought these characters to life in a way that far exceeded all my hopes and dreams. My friends and family, for your honesty and feedback and your unconditional love and support. To Claire: your heart is so big, sometimes I can hardly believe I get to share so much of it—thank you for listening to every poem, idea, doubt, and worry and for being a voice of encouragement and reason.

Finally, to my loyal readers: I wrote this book as part of my healing. I like to think it is a testament to how far I have come in the face of a battle I had not expected. For far too long, I remained in the shadows, trading my sense of self and worth for someone who was hardly worth it, and it very nearly destroyed me. But it didn't. Because I did rise again, and wherever you are and the things that have happened to you, I know in my heart you will rise from the ashes again too.

Instagram: @courtneypeppernell
TikTok: @courtneypeppernell
Twitter: @CourtPeppernell
Email: courtney@pepperbooks.org

www.peppernell.com

On the outskirts of a forest with evergreen trees, beyond the mountain range with snow and ice, and skies filled with spirits ancient and wise, lived soul guides of a different kind. With emerald eyes burning bright, and made from spark and flame, with hearts filled with compassion and courage, their purpose is to remind us of all we can reclaim. They appear to us in moments of dire need, a light in the darkness, a glimmer of unexpected truth, and a hand to hold until we are freed. When one feels as though life has been burned to the ground, left in piles of ash, someone is always here to remind us that life begins again, despite how hard we fall and how disastrous the crash.

On one such day, while walking through the forest, the sun beating down from above, thinking of the days ahead, and filled with love, the guide found a phoenix, broken and in despair, shedding an old life, and in desperate need of repair. The phoenix was you, and this is your story of redemption and starting anew.

The world felt like it had ended, and there was nowhere else to go, so alone in the woods, facing the darkest night, the guide looked upon you, a burning light, to remind you that life was always worth the fight.

Out of the Ashes

"There you are," the guide said, "It's time to start again."

"But how can I," you replied, "when all I feel is ache and pain?"

And the guide looked solemn, as though it understood that, when we are betrayed, it can feel as though the world has been drained of all its good.

"Where can I go, when every memory aches, when all I feel is empty, a shadow of a person that constantly breaks?"

The guide looked back at you, with kindness and understanding, "My friend," they replied, "sometimes life brings us burdens too hurtful to bear, and we are dealt cards that are truly unfair."

"So, what do I do," you asked, "to find my way back, when everything feels terrifying, and I've lost all that I knew?"

The guide replied, "We must break down, and turn to ash, so that we can begin once more, for all beautiful things rise again, better and stronger than they were before."

You were hesitant to let go, unsure if turning to ash meant destroying all that you had known, but in the depths of a beating forest, you realized that, sometimes, to tear yourself down is to relearn all that you are and finally be found. Through the process, you learned that destruction leads to the end, but this does not mean you cannot build again. That in the quiet and stillness, we are reminded of all the things that make us strong, and this leads to transformation, and reasons to belong. You learned you will always rise, with far more courage than you thought you had, and you will undoubtedly overcome all the things that made you sad. Your resurgence sparked a blaze you long thought had extinguished, and you understood through time all burdens are relinquished.

When you rose, the color returned to the sky, in brilliant bursts of vibrant hues, and the world lit up in song, celebrating a brighter and stronger you, embracing the beauty and strength you have embodied all along. There you were, reborn and surrounded in renewal, gracious in all your feelings—an enlightened purpose to start again, full of hope and new beginnings. And while, in life, we are broken, and fall many times, experiencing hardship and fears that sometimes force us to surrender and hide, the truth is found every time we pause, for the fire in our heart will never be diminished and will always burn deep inside, never to be extinguished.

# How to rise from the Ashes

resilience

hope

courage

determination

growth

acknowledgment

*The process through . . .*

THE DESTRUCTION   1

THE END   31

THE QUIET   61

THE WRATH   89

THE TRANSFORMATION   117

THE ARISING   147

THE RESURGENCE   177

*. . . you will rise from the ashes*

Whether it is a day or a week or an entire year, the things that have hurt you and destroyed your confidence and sense of worth are not measured by anyone or anything other than you. The scars that have been left behind are your wounds. You are the person who sees them, feels them, and wears them. It is your hands that wrap around your heart and acknowledge its pain. It is your mind that finds the resolve, your soul that permits yourself the grace to heal. You're the one who understands your heartache, as much as you are the one who has the resilience to overcome it.

Courtney Peppernell

The phoenix ignites—
feathers unraveling with flame.
The fire consumes the old self,
as the ash falls in silence.
But in such stillness
remains the beat of a heart.
There is something stirring,
not yet ready,
but waiting.

That was just it; I did not think
I would see heartache again.

We had crossed paths many times before,
but not like this.

So, when it opened my door, and it walked
into the home I had spent all this time building,
I could hardly believe it was true.

"How could it be," I asked, "after all this time?"

And heartache bowed its head. "I'm sorry," it said.
"I can hardly believe it too."

—how could I be so wrong about forever?

This is what I had always known,
that I would have recognized you anywhere—
your eyes, your smile, the wave in your hair.

But these days, the memory of you is fading.

Soon, you will just be nothing.

# Out of the Ashes

Sometimes I wonder if you remember
the way I looked at you, as though you
were made of gold.

It does not make any sense to me, the way
someone could treat the person they are
meant to love as though they are nothing
more than dirt on the bottom of their shoe.

But the truth is, you were never the treasure—
I was.

Courtney Peppernell

How strange it is
that, once upon a time,
I could never imagine
what it would be
to not know you—
and now
I wish I had never met you.

## Out of the Ashes

"She adores you," or so people would say.
"She loves you so deeply," or so people
would believe.

But the truth is, you don't do the things
you did to me to someone you cherish.

All I was to you was someone to take
advantage of, someone you sucked the life
out of, until you had no use for it anymore.

You're a parasite, always have been, always will be.

This is what destroyed me the most—it was not the cheating, the leaving, or the betrayal. It was that you had no guilt and no remorse. You looked into my eyes—windows to my soul—and you lied. Day in and day out. You slept soundly, you continued to take from me, you lived in this house, carved memories with the people in our lives, and you did not for a single moment have an ounce of shame for your actions. My heart was a home, and you were the truck that drove right through it.

## Out of the Ashes

This is what I learned from
the way I was treated by you.

I was told that I was not worth
the effort.

I was not your choice, nor was
the life and the home I had so
patiently and carefully built.

I was betrayed by you more than
I have ever been betrayed by anyone
in my entire life—
and you were meant to love me.

Once upon a time,
we said that we would follow
each other anywhere,
that I would go to the end
of the earth for you,
and you for me,
that we had loved
one another's soul
in every life—

the cruelest part
is that I had meant it
but that you had not.

# Out of the Ashes

Sometimes, in more fragile moments,
I close my eyes and I return to my old life.
I play it back like an old movie, scene by scene.
And I am reminded of why it no longer fits.

I did grieve you, or rather I grieved
the version of you I thought I knew.

It felt as though that person had died,
and I suppose, in some ways, they had.

Because, as it turned out, they'd only
ever existed in the parts of my heart
that so badly wanted them to be true.

I wanted you to be kind; I wanted you
to be thoughtful; I wanted you to be
supportive and wonderful and a partner
capable of keeping me safe—
but you were none of these things,
and you never had been.

I mourned what I thought you were,
more than anything.

## Out of the Ashes

They would look at me
with light eyes and a gentle
smile and say, "Look how far
you've come in moving on"—
while I was still knee-deep
in rubble and living with
a scream inside me
that only I could hear.

You came home one day and simply said,
"I do not love you anymore."

And what followed was insurmountable
grief.

My heart has withstood many storms before—
but you were an F5.

*CATACLYSMIC*

There are so many things that are impacted
by infidelity and by severing a vow.

There I was, and I had been decimated.
I hardly knew how I was going to continue.

But I did.

It took everything, but I rebuilt.

And the irony is that I needed my entire
world to be blown to shreds; I needed it
all to be blown away—so that I could see the light.

You were so wrong for me.

## Out of the Ashes

Once, I spent all night holding you,
and now my arms have been empty
for longer than I knew you.

Time turned us into strangers.

The world became a different place after the loss—color faded, the air felt different, the absence echoed through the shadows. I was exploring unknown territory with unfamiliar hues. In every corner, the loneliness called, haunting my every move. And it was the pain of unanswered questions, conversations that were never finished, whispers of what had been that would never be again that kept me up all night long. When you are betrayed by someone you love, it brings about the kind of destruction that breaks your soul apart. And yet, as you lie there, slowly withering away, the smallest flower in a storm of darkness, there comes a day when you look to the sky and you feel the sun.

Out of the Ashes

If I had a time machine, and the me from seven years ago landed in my living room, I've often wondered what I would say. Would I tell her that I was sorry? I wish she knew back then what I know now. We could have saved so much pain. We could have saved so much time. Avoided the hurt, the cost, the seams being ripped and torn apart. But then, I wonder, if she hadn't gone through all she had survived, would I still be me? So perhaps, I suppose, if I had a time machine, and I could talk to past me, I'd instead tell her, "You're going to make it to today."

I know, you gave your heart to the wrong person.

I did too.

You feel embarrassed, ashamed, completely alone.
You wonder what you did wrong.
You cannot believe you didn't see all the signs sooner.
How did this happen—how could I have gotten
everything so wrong?

But it wasn't you.

Just remember that the selfish prey on the kind.

So, this is what you do—you rise, you plant yourself firmly
on the ground,
you press the soles of heels so deeply into the earth that you
feel its power.

And you say to yourself, *I am worth more than they
ever deserved.*

Out of the Ashes

It was an ordinary day. I was washing dishes, and my momma was having tea at the dining table. We were talking because I always talk to my momma. And she said to me, "I know you feel as though you have lost everything right now. I know you feel as though your entire life has been ripped from you, and in a lot of ways, it has, but the one thing that has not been taken from you is your ability to love, truly, wholeheartedly, from the depths of your soul. The person who broke your heart will never have depth. You will move on; you will be happy again. But they'll never have that happiness. They will always repeat the same patterns in their life, because they are selfish and incapable of truly loving someone. But you—you find joy in the deep."

All you did was take, and take, and take. You were like poison, spreading through my body, trying to destroy the life inside me. And at first, I questioned myself. It was my fault for giving too much. I was to blame for never setting boundaries and for allowing you to walk all over me. And in the darkness of the night, the tears filled my pillow, and I swore to the stars I would board up my heart forever. But the stars spoke back. They said to me, "Just because you have crossed paths with a monster does not mean your heart should change. Give, because giving is beautiful. Love, because loving is rewarding. Evolve, because evolving is healing. Remaining true to who you are, despite the way someone has treated you, is power."

# Out of the Ashes

There was a time when I would reflect
on all the things I had said of love
and all the words I had dedicated to her,
and I would feel deep regret.

For when someone betrays your trust,
they destroy the way you speak of them.

There was no longer love in my pen, only grief.
There was no longer devotion in every sentence,
but rather shame.

She was a scorch mark on every page.

But I see things differently now.
Because the way I talked of love was genuine—
it was real for me, even though it had been given
to someone who never should have had it.

And for this reason, I also know that you can
reclaim words.

They can take on new meanings, and they can
be something to someone again.

—I take back all those poems I wrote for her

Courtney Peppernell

If I could talk to my heart,
I would say, *Forgive me*
*for every beat that was wasted—*
*I let us love the wrong person.*

When you have been cheated on, it takes everything to see it as a lesson rather than something that almost destroys you. It's true, it breaks your trust in ways hard to imagine. It's a ripple effect. A crack in your heart that spreads and impacts so many other things in your life. And I know you will sit in your thoughts, and you will hurt, and you will wonder whether there is anyone out there who would never betray you like that—*Where are they? Do they exist? How will I ever trust again?* And all you need to do is look in the mirror. You didn't cheat. You were faithful, and honest, and committed. And if you exist, then there is someone out there, just as genuine as you, wondering if you exist too.

We drove from state to state, singing at the top of our lungs. But now I can barely listen to those songs without my heart going dark. There's space between us now, wide as the sky we once sat under, dreaming about all the things we wanted. I see pictures of you, and it's strange—there's my best friend, but you're surrounded by faces I don't know, living a life I'm not part of, writing a story I'm not in. It destroys me, the way I don't know you anymore. Somehow, we got lost—like the songs we forgot how to sing together. I don't know how else to say it; I never meant for us to break, I miss my friend more than anything, can't we just go back?

## Out of the Ashes

I thought I knew the things
that could destroy me—
things like failed relationships
and lost opportunities.
Being lied to or bullied.
Feeling lost or watching
my worth walk out the door.

But then I lost my dog.

My heart's never known
that kind of pain.

To be destroyed is to feel as though the entire world has crumbled down around you, as though you are holding your own soul in your hands and watching it disintegrate before your very eyes. It is a moment when time stands still, when your chest feels heavy, when you want to scream but no sound comes from your mouth. The dreams you had, gone. The hopes you had, dashed. The love you devoted yourself to, abandoned. Everything you thought you knew now lies shattered at your feet. It brings darkness; suffocation; a deep, haunting void. But despite the ruin, there is still a seed. And that seed will whisper to you that, despite your grief, you must climb upward. Through the darkness, toward the light, as all seeds do. Climb and climb and climb, and eventually you will breathe the fresh air and find the sunlight.

Out of the Ashes

As I sat in the rubble, I wondered how I would ever find the strength to sift through it. But every day I worked through the ache, you were there. I need you to know that having a friend like you made it so much easier to find a way forward. Every time you checked in, even on the days I didn't have the strength to reply, gave me hope—there was someone out there thinking of me, and that means more than I'll ever be able to tell you. Thank you for being there, for all the long drives, for the conversations, for breathing laughter back into my life, for the shoulder to lean on when I was falling apart. You were the lighthouse I needed to find my way back home.

The grief nearly destroyed me, and the loss broke me in every way. It was as relentless as it was fleeting; one moment, I was sure I could see the light in front of me, and the next, nothing but shadow. It ravaged my heart, and the very core of who I was had been irreversibly changed. The wake of such agony left no stone of me unturned; it spared no corner of my mind from its touch. It took many forms—boxing your belongings, your birthday, our anniversary, perfume that still lingered, an empty house, the final papers—and it shook the foundations of my life. Heartache reigned during that era; it sat upon its throne and it demanded I bow down, despite all of my efforts to run. But in all the destruction, chaos, and profound sadness, amid the ruins, there were seeds of resilience, and they took root. Small at first, but, in time, they grew. Until, one day, out of the rubble, I emerged—taller than I had been, stronger than I had thought I was, lessons learned, and perspective gained. And while I knew I would carry scars, I also knew they were reminders of a chapter I had survived.

—I survived you

# Out of the Ashes

I vowed
once in a lifetime.
But you had your
fingers crossed
behind your back.

Courtney Peppernell

We will never go through life
without something ending—
losing someone we love,
an opportunity that sailed by,
a dream that slipped through
our fingers.

And while these endings are painful,
and you might feel like the sky
collapsed on top of you, they also
carve out a space to start over.

Endings teach us what remain;
they each thread their way into a
bigger story, one where strength
is sewn into every lesson.

Out of the Ashes

For so long, I just couldn't seem to slow the thoughts down, as they raced over each other one after the other, like a continuous cycle. These thoughts were fast, chaotic, and messy, like the way a current flows after weeks and weeks of rain; or a bustling city in rush hour, with honking horns and moving bodies; a dam breaking or a house burning to the ground. The never-ending rumination was enough to undo me—I felt trapped in my own head. In those moments, calm felt unattainable, it was so hard to sleep, conversations were disjointed, and I was almost always somewhere else. Someone tells you they struggle to be here, and you often wonder why, but in those moments, with those thoughts pounding in my head, I finally understood. And I am not saying an end is the answer; I am just saying I get it.

"Where do you go,
when you disappear?"

To a place I can see myself,
and I tell her time and time again—
this is not the end.

You said you would love me until the very end. But the end never arrived because you left me halfway through forever. And I must have asked myself one hundred times, *Does anything ever last anymore?* What hope was there if forever is promised and never fulfilled. But then I am reminded of the sun and how it has warmed the earth since the dawn of time, or how Hachikō waited for the train every day for years and years, or the way elephants stay with the body of their fallen long after they are gone. There are things that are enduring and everlasting, and I know that I deserve to be loved until the very end.

It was sometime in autumn's golden haze when
you walked into my life and changed everything.

If I'd known back then what I know now,
I wonder whether I would have done anything differently—
maybe said more or less, I am not sure.

In the stillness, I am engulfed in memory
as it twists around my heart in agony.
I imagine the lives we would have led
if it all hadn't ended.

Time creates a divide between us,
further and further.

And I am constantly reminded, what would
I have done had I known it would be the last time?

# Out of the Ashes

I grappled with the idea
that everything had already
been pre-written.

Had this pain always been
meant for me?
Had the hurt always been
destined to arrive at my
sleepy little door?
Was every chapter mapped
out before I had even known?

And I wanted to ask the universe—
"Why did you write it so?"

For seasons change, and so do we;
a page is turned, leaving nothing
but memory.

There I was, and I was so afraid
of everything falling apart
that I had completely overlooked
the fact none of it had been glued
together properly in the first place.
I was so afraid that they would leave,
I didn't pay attention to myself leaving first.

Out of the Ashes

Life was not over just because the pace changed. It is true I had been handed an unexpected path, filled with challenges. It seemed my world was unfolding all around me in a way I had never intended. I carried shame for the way everyone else around me seemed to have it so fiercely put together: success, families, poignancy. While I, now in my thirties, had just had my heart obliterated. But this is the thing about neat packages: the contents have often been jumbled all around inside—you just cannot see. So, I embraced my new messy. I decided that, even in the absolute devastation, I would find a way to make an end, a new beginning.

That was the most important thing I learned—I had to stop expecting loyalty, devotion, and empathy from someone who couldn't even give me basic honesty. I had to grow into that knowledge, to listen to what I deserved and what I needed, and I had to respect myself enough to do it.

That was the difference;
my love for you would
have lasted forever—
yours, for me, expired.

Courtney Peppernell

I see your shadow everywhere,
finding reminders of you
in every corner of my day.

And I know I'm supposed
to wish you the best,
but you're the one who left.

I can't sleep without hearing
all the things you used to say—
"I will love you for all of time."
It was never meant to be this way.

And I know I'm supposed
to wish you the best,
but you're the one who left.

Did you know my heart would break?
How can I forgive you now,
when you have brought such ache?

And I know I'm supposed
to wish you the best,
but you're the one who left.

When all was said and done, the lesson I learned was that I could not change someone, despite how many chances I gave them or how many times I suppressed my frustration and disappointment, hoping they would do better. I had justified their toxic behavior and disrespect of all my own boundaries because I truly believed they would change. But I was wrong—I could not make them selfless; I could not make them kind; I could not make them empathetic, accountable, or able to see how their actions impacted other people. I could not make them the person who returned the shopping cart, the person who held my hand or calmed me through every storm. There's no changing a wolf, even if they wear sheep's clothing.

Courtney Peppernell

I wanted the happy ending;
I wanted the ever after,
and I truly thought I had it.

But life isn't a fairy tale,
wrapped in a neat bow.
The truth is—stories change.

For the longest time, I tried
to outrun the grief of it all,
to escape the breaking.
But it only prolonged the hurt.

For the truth was also this—
a different ending does not
mean the end of you.

The meaning and the story
is in the journey itself.

## Out of the Ashes

We unfolded the way all stories do—
we had a beginning, a middle, and an end.

The saddest part was that I never wanted
to put the book down.

Courtney Peppernell

I was ready to throw life away—
every single part of it.

I was out of my mind with grief.

It was as though I had begun
with a landscape meant for dreams,
love, aspirations, and moments
of joy, and in a single choice,
you had blown it all to bits.

You sent my mind into lockdown,
unable to escape the way you haunted
every building.

I was leasing my peace to the memory
of the past, rather than reclaiming
the space.

And if I continued this way, then there
would be no room for growth.

So, I evicted you.

It was almost enough to turn me bitter, a cold, harsh fact—bad things happen to good people. And I couldn't understand. I had always followed the rules, right from the very beginning. I turned my homework in on time, I listened to instructions, I held open doors, I returned lost wallets, I was always generous with my time, my love, my money. I only crossed the street on green, I always put the shopping cart back, I lived my life always trying to choose goodness. Yet, in return, the universe had dealt me a truly awful card. This was my reward? This was the play the universe had made? But it didn't matter; the truth is painful. Good people get handed bad cards, over and over again. It was always going to boil down to what I did with those cards—and I chose to continue on.

This is what an ending does to you—
it turns your life colorless.

It will feel as though you have
lost everything.

And you must feel this way.

You need to live in the gray
so that, eventually,
when the color returns,
you will find the beauty
in its vibrance.

## Out of the Ashes

You were right;
we were two different people,
right from the very start.

We were different in the way that
you were the rock and I was the jewel.
I was kind and you were cruel.

I had spent my life making myself smaller. Trying to shrink myself so that nobody would notice me. When I walked into a room, I disappeared into the crowd. When I spoke, the words were soft. I have tried to make myself quiet, prioritize others, consider their needs greater than my own. And it has only caused immense suffering. Did I really think so little of myself that I allowed others to walk all over me without protest? Did I not believe I was worth so much more? The tide has changed. I opened my eyes one day, and I said, *No more.* There would be no more shrinking, there would be no more disappearing or avoiding. Because I do fill space, and that space matters.

Out of the Ashes

You didn't see it coming. Because you believed in every word they ever said. You trusted that word, like you trusted them. And when it shattered all around you, so did your heart. For how could you possibly trust anyone ever again after the person you trusted the most could turn around and lie to you so easily? This is the thing about words—they are beautiful, and they carry worth, but they are also meaningless without action. You need to listen to the words being spoken, and you need to see them being actioned.

Of course, life went on. The leaves fell, the buses continued running, the tide surged and receded. People all around me kept moving. Time did not stop. And yet I plunged myself into darkness. In the darkness, I had so many regrets—*I wish we had never met, I wish I hadn't ignored my intuition so many damn times, I wish I had never given my soul to you*—it was all a disaster. You had been the grenade and obliterated all that I thought I knew of love. I enveloped myself in darkness for so long that when the sun suddenly shone one day, I hardly recognized it. But it felt so familiar, so warm. And I realized that, even in the moments when it feels like I cannot move forward, the sun still rises, and it still sets. It's always going to be there.

Out of the Ashes

I have tried to count every time we ended,
because we ended many times.

Our communication ended; you no longer
wanted to hold my hand, or me;
my faith in you ended; my worth to you ended;
my trust in you ended.

And with every ending, a piece of me seemed
to break away.

Courtney Peppernell

There will be a time in your life
when you will be hurt more than
you have ever known.

You will consider that the end—
and it will be.

It will be the end of you.

For you will never be the same again.

But there is hope in this,
because you will grow.

## Out of the Ashes

I wanted to ask you—
would you feel the same
if you knew I was broken?

I miss my friend; it's like
I've lost one hundred pieces
of myself.

I see parts of you
in every new person I meet.

But it's not the same.

It's been so long, and I trace back
all the times we shared.

When we lived in moments
that felt like they'd last forever.

If I texted you, would you reply?

The betrayal altered the way I saw love;
where it was once vibrant and full of life,
something I embraced wholeheartedly,
it had been tainted by the way I had been
treated: unfairly, cruelly, horrendously.

And I grieved it—the color of it all.

For I now had this darkened idea of love.
As though it were some monstrous thing,
never to be trusted or opened to again.

Until, one day, Love came to me, full of
earnest possibility and promise.

I, of course, hesitated, unsure and afraid.

And Love said to me, "You never really
knew me, but one day you will."

*One day*, I thought.

And unexpectedly, "one day" arrived.

The ending changed, and so did your path. Suddenly, the road was not paved out before you, the stepping-stones were muddled, there was no clear way forward; these are the kinds of things that can shatter a person. So, when the thoughts are keeping you up all night, remember this—you are more than capable of loving what you see in the mirror again, opening your heart up to love once more, healing from the damage someone else caused, accepting new dreams, understanding that failure only leaves room for lessons, looking at this change and hoping for the best. That you can grow in new directions and be at peace with all the new ways you are evolving. That even though it feels like time has been stolen from you, there is still so much more of it left. You will overcome the shadows to see the light, you will meet with hope once more, and you will find joy in the space between the stars. Yes, the ending changed, but it is filled with possibility.

I used to think healing would feel like revenge, but it doesn't—it just feels like breathing again. I hung the mirror—the one you hated—in the hallway. I changed the rugs in the living room; there are more plants in the house; I adopted the dog you said we could never have. My hair is shorter since you left; I changed the color. I can hike for hours on end; I'm healthier; I let the air back into my lungs instead of holding my breath every hour around you. People say my eyes aren't sad anymore; they're alive, connected, engaged. I no longer walk with my head down; my heart feels lighter, not as heavy. I'm taking chances on all the things you told me I couldn't do; I am freeing myself of all the ways you made me feel small. There are days when I imagine an alternate ending—we are still together, and I am still the same: invisible. If it were a movie, I wouldn't watch it. If it were a book, I wouldn't read it. You froze me in time, and I fell for the illusion of you—but I'm alive again; I'm alive again.

## Out of the Ashes

This is what it means to be the phoenix:
you end and then you rise again.

But in between, you must sit and reflect
in the quiet.

Before I could rise,
I needed to live in the dust.

I needed to be broken
all the way apart
so that I could examine
every fragment and choose
how they would
be reconstructed.

And I wondered how I was
ever going to find the courage
to begin that process.

Until, one day, in a home
by the ocean, I saw whales
breaching on the horizon,
it was a still, cloudy day.

Those whales reminded me
that hope existed, even in
the stillness of the sea.

## Out of the Ashes

There were so many things
I wish I had told you—
so many more moments
I wish we'd had.

That's the saddest part;
you always wish you had
more time.

Now I whisper these things in the
middle of the night, hoping
the quiet will carry them
to wherever you are.

Courtney Peppernell

Loss leaves a quiet trail behind it,
a path where memories softly fade—
where the heart still feels the weight
of words unsaid and love that stayed.

## Out of the Ashes

I miss you in the quieter moments of life,
right as the sun is rising, or when I am
waiting at the traffic lights, or walking
the trail just beyond the house.

I miss you in the soft light of the moon,
as I stare at the ceiling during the night,
or when I order from our favorite café
and it is one coffee instead of two.

I miss you in all this sweet, tender silence,
but it's the loudest feeling in my heart.

The world constantly tells us to look on the bright side of everything. This can distract from pain, from anger, from frustration—all equally needed feelings—if you are hurt, then you are hurt and allowed to be so. Sometimes even those closest to us hurt us. There is no bright side to this, no positive spin. If you have been hurt, then you must feel that pain deep in your heart and in your bones. You must weather that anger and that frustration to feel valid in your hurt so that it may pass.

Out of the Ashes

Have you noticed today the soft light of a quiet morning,
or the birdsong melody so intricate and sweet,
the way they call to the world, right there on your street?

Have you noticed today the way the leaves dance in
    the breeze,
whispering stories of yesterday through the tallest of trees?
A butterfly fluttering by, with patterned wings in
    colorful hues,
a soft and delicate journey, across a sky so blue?

Have you noticed today a handwritten letter, inked
    with careful
thought, carrying love and memory in each line
    it's wrought?
The first sip of coffee on a crisp fall day, waking the
    soul gently
in the warmest of ways?

Have you noticed today how easily small things
    are overseen,
too preoccupied with where we are going and where we
    have been?
In all the rushing, there and about, it is easy to forget,
the magic exists when we pause and take a breath.

Courtney Peppernell

The days were long and difficult.
There was always this brief moment
in the morning when I'd rise and the world
would still be quiet, the sun barely
yet risen over the hill.

And I had hope in those moments.
I felt safe; the weight in my chest
wasn't as heavy.

But then it would vanish, and I would
barely get through the day.

I wish I could bottle those first moments.

*Out of the Ashes*

The most difficult part about choosing silence was that I still had so many questions. I wanted to ask you, "In the moments when you were unfaithful, did you ever stop to think of what it would do to me—to the person who had loved you unconditionally? Did you ever stop to think of the ways in which this would devastate me?"

At the same time, I found my answers in the quiet—you never would have told me the truth anyway; you would have lied and lied and lied. Because our history had always been based on your lies, your falseness, your trickery.

The silence told me the truth—you never actually cared.

Courtney Peppernell

I did not want to face it,
the quiet depths of my despair.

But I told fear to step aside
so that I could listen to the hurt.
And it led me to healing.

## Out of the Ashes

And now I look at my hands and they are aging;
I look at my body and it has changed shape;
I look at my fingers and count all the ways
I should have seen it coming.

Was I a fool to have placed my trust, my heart,
my soul into the wrong hands?

I tried to keep pretending, carry on the facade,
as though love did not blind me, as though
I had always seen.

But I had been blind.

It took an entire earthquake, walls tumbling,
paint stripped, rose-colored glasses smashed
into a million pieces, for me to finally see.

And I saw, and I wept, and I weathered the storm.

My new war is with myself, in the moments I am alone,
and the shame plagues me—I should have known;
I should have seen it; I should have walked away sooner.

Courtney Peppernell

I was on an open road, a long stretch of emptiness in front of me. And I felt nothing. I was filled with only darkness. *Is this what life is—a long road of silence?* The miles wore on and on, and slowly the horizon began to transform. The dawn was distant, but it was arriving. And so the silence changed. Perhaps this was what the nothingness taught me. I was not fleeing the dark but rather driving toward the light. And I understood on that road, way out in the middle of nothing, that no night, no matter how dark, could refuse the rise of the sun.

## Out of the Ashes

The betrayal lingers, even long after it's happened. It weaves its way into everything you do. You'll spend hours comparing yourself with everyone else. You will look at yourself, and you will think of yourself as this hideous thing. If the person you loved could cheat on you, discard you, break you in a such a horrific, callous way, then surely someone else could do that too.

The quiet will eat away at your soul, so many questions, so few answers; there is nowhere to escape the ruminating.

But let me tell you about the kindness of others—my friends cooked me dinner, my mother would send sunflowers, my neighbor would leave letters in my mailbox, the barista at my favorite café would always draw a smile on my coffee cup.

And it took a long time to accept such kindness, but that is what got me through, for those little acts of love reminded me there was hope in all the quiet.

Courtney Peppernell

Hold on to the stillness;
it will teach you to see people
for who they are and not
what you want them to be.

It will remind you
when someone shows you
who they really are—
believe them.

It is often clarity that evades us in the chaos of every day. We search for it in all the wrong places—instant gratification, distraction, avoidance—and we wonder why we never find the answer. But the truth is, the answers are in the quiet. They are here when we have slowed down and turned off the noise, when we have the space to breathe, to listen to the way our heart beats. Do you not hear the answer in every beat? It says to you, "Life begins and ends in the quiet."

Courtney Peppernell

Self-care is listening to the quiet,
even if it feels as though you are
buried under tons and tons of rubble—
anguish, guilt, shame, fear, heartache—
because it is by listening to the quiet
that we can hear our soul.

It will call for us, demanding time
and space to heal, reflect, and grow.

## Out of the Ashes

It took me years to understand,
the silence is not the absence of noise.

It is a presence itself.

It is loud and demanding, but it is also
a friend of comfort, an understanding
without judgment.

The silence says to you in the
middle of the night, "It is not too late;
you can start over."

Sometimes the sheer desperation for change will steal the breath from your lungs. And alongside it, the ache for acceptance will weigh heavily in your heart. You will wonder how you are ever supposed to escape the void. After all, you created it, this gaping, dark, never-ending hole in your soul. It's your fault. At least this is what the thoughts will tell you, endlessly, until you have convinced yourself time is standing still. But time is not standing still; it is constantly moving, and so are you. So, in the breath you take, right before the thought, remember, it doesn't matter if you are having the best week of your life or the worst; the most important thing you can do is show up for both.

## Out of the Ashes

The stillness speaks in the softest tone,
a reassuring song that's all its own—
in every pause, a chance to see,
the simple magic of just to be.

The journey is unfolding—like a flower in bloom, a sunrise over the sea, a map headed to where you want to be. When you are hurt enough times, your heart boards itself up. And then, one day, you find enough courage to open the door, only a crack at first, but then, slowly, it's all the way open, and the sunlight is pouring into the room. And you find your best sweater and your favorite shoes, and you're tying your shoelaces, and you are telling yourself, *I can do this, one step at a time. I am here, I am still here.*

Life is the book, and time is the pages, moving through every chapter of your story. You will learn that you don't get to choose the plot, only how you respond to it. There are things that will happen in your story that you never saw coming, and they will interrupt your life in ways you never imagined. Pain changes people—this is a hard truth, a lesson learned by many. Through pain, and suffering, you understand more about yourself and those you surround yourself with. Suffering shapes you; it alters the way you look at the world and your ability to continue forward. And often people suffer in silence. So, if the quiet is too dark today, remember this—every chapter ends; the suffering will end.

If anything, the proof is in the number of times I sat in my driveway too afraid to walk into an empty home. Last year, it was too many times to count. I would sit in my driveway and fight the urge to open the car door. It was not a home anymore. It had been destroyed. But now, I pull in, and the light is on inside. And I don't lose my breath every time I walk through the front door.

Yes, the quiet is daunting. When there are no distractions, you are forced to reflect. And when you are reflecting, your thoughts can turn into the runaway truck, plummeting toward the cliff edge. You are filled with all sorts of dreaded fears—*How will I find my way back? I don't know where I am headed. Things are falling apart, and what if it gets worse? Am I stupid? Do others think less of me because I can never seem to do anything right?*—and before you know it, the land beneath you has slipped so far downhill, you are staring up at a mountain and wondering how you are ever going to climb it again. Do you not understand? You are supposed to be the driver. You lose control because you are allowing the fear to drive.

There is no such thing as a time machine. You cannot go back and alter the steps you have already taken. There is no changing what has already happened. But there is a bridge between the past and the future, and it is called reflection. And when you stand on this bridge, you can honor where you have been as well as map the course on which you wish to go. It is here, standing still, where you will find your breath.

## Out of the Ashes

Perhaps this is the most beautiful thing
about our thoughts—
they change, they evolve, and they grow.

Years ago, I thought differently;
years from now, I'll think differently too.

All I know is that continuing to think and to feel
is the surest way of making it through.

Courtney Peppernell

To take the first step
is always the hardest.

When you are challenged,
the walk forward becomes
tentative, unsure.

Your soul is exhausted, weary
that the scars you bear will
change your outlook on the world—
and they will; you will forever
be changed, but you are not
forever broken.

Your determination will find
its way back to you; it will
breathe new life into your heart,
and with this new life,
you will find your spark once more.

Out of the Ashes

When the dust had settled,
and the shock had subsided,
there were long days of anger,
of rage, of absolute fury.

For I had finally woken the
fuck up.

I was alive for the first time.

I was acutely aware of the fool
I had been taken for.

Of all the ways I had been deceived.

Oh,

How that stirs a fire

and how it can burn

and burn and burn.

The anger that I carried was not just my own—but for the child I once was. That innocent and trusting part of me who believed love was safe, who didn't yet know all the ways someone could lie and take advantage of her. She had been hurt, discarded, and disregarded, as well. And so, for her, I stood my ground. I used my anger to move forward; never again would I allow anybody to treat me in the way the monster I had loved had treated me.

## Out of the Ashes

In my anger, the world narrowed—
my vision tunneled, thoughts sharpened
like razors, and my heart pounded
with relentless primal beats.

Everything and everyone was a threat.

I had been undervalued, overlooked,
and abandoned, in the cruelest way possible.

And it awoke a long-dormant volcano.

The grief was easy to talk about—I knew I was sad, I knew I was hurt, I could talk about the pain all day long. But it was the anger that scared me. Because I found it difficult to weave, it would get away from me, and a small spark would turn into a raging wildfire that I could not master. And it didn't matter how many deep breaths I took or how many times I tried to reason with it all; the anger would take ahold of me. It would shake me around and get the better of me. The anger became a dragon, untamed, fierce and unyielding. And yet, in the moments the dragon was alone, it would weep, fearful that all this fury would change its softness. This being said, my anger helped me survive.

Out of the Ashes

There are still some moments
when I cannot fathom that
a person like you exists.

Someone so selfish and arrogant
and only interested in what they
can gain and not what they can give.

What a miserable existence you live—
how grateful I am to be free of you.

You reveled in all your dishonesty;
you thrived on manipulation, always
weaving webs and webs of lies.

I once saw the world through your eyes;
I was blinded by love, but now I truly see
all your emptiness within.

The mask you wore so well crumbled
under the weight of your ego.
It revealed your hollow shell,
someone incapable of genuine love.

And for that, I hope you rot in hell.

In the prison of your own making,
haunted by screams of your betrayal,
may you find no solace and no peace.

Courtney Peppernell

Because I have found my freedom,
and in that I find my strength.
While you remain trapped forever
in the misery of your own deceit.

You made me sick—the mere thought of you.
I shuddered every time I had to speak your name.
I hoped, begged, demanded that all the suffering
in the world be redirected at you.

That is what you deserved.
Absolute misery.

I wanted you to feel all the pain, the humiliation,
and the suffering you had brought upon me.

There was nothing in this world that I wanted more
than for you to disappear into a giant black hole
and never see the light of day again.

But then, one day, I realized you *were* suffering—
because you were you.

You were already empty, unfulfilled, and chasing
a false reality. You didn't have the capacity to truly
love someone or hold any sort of honest virtue.

You would suffer enough just by being you.

It was always very different behind closed doors. She would hurt me, and I would try to tell her so, to talk through it. But it only ever made it worse. I would be diminished, until I was nothing more than dust on the floor. I was told I was too sensitive, that I couldn't take a joke, that my reaction to unkind behavior was my fault. And it created the kind of fog in my mind that is difficult to see through—Was I too sensitive? Did I take things too seriously? Was it all my fault?

Until, one day, I recognized the abuse. It was subtle, covert, almost undetected, but it was there. It was there in the way she would always raise her voice; it was there in the way she would humiliate me in front of people; it was there in the way she would cheat, lie, and demand things from me.

And I was so angry about it for the longest time. How could I have not seen? How could I have not left sooner? Why the fuck did I stay with her for so many years? The shame and rage burned a hole right through my heart.

There is a long gap in my life now. It is not as though I will look back on those years fondly. They are tainted, and I will never forgive her for that—but I don't have to.

I must forgive myself.

That forgiveness started with shredding all the photos. I took them one by one, and I put them through that shredder. I shredded my old life, the one to which I was chained, and I have never felt freer.

The thing about rage is that it is not a solitary feeling. It usually arrives on your doorstep because fear, shame, misery, and distress have invited it over. And together they will unleash destruction on your life. Anger is fire; it can both illuminate and devastate. In your deepest moments of anger, it will feel like you are battling a force far greater than yourself. Until the day you realize it is because anger demands to be acknowledged—only then will balance arrive at your door, and the destruction will no longer consume you.

Courtney Peppernell

You knew what you were doing
and how much it would destroy her,
and you continued doing it anyway.

That is the type of person you are—
someone who cares for nobody
except themselves.

All you had to do was treat her well,
and you couldn't even manage that.

# Out of the Ashes

The anger, just like fire,
can either light your way
or burn you down—
it depends on how you
tend to the flame.

Courtney Peppernell

May your deception rot in your throat
while I continue to reclaim my life.
I will rise from the ashes you left,
and I will be stronger, wiser, and freer.
All the while, you will drown in your lies
and the mess you have made, and I hope
it haunts you every goddamn day.

## Out of the Ashes

There is nothing amicable
about the way you
tore our lives in two.

There is no denying the
colossal damage you caused.

And perhaps the worst part
is the false narrative you've spun.
"We are two different people who
grew apart."

How convenient for you,
in the face of the real story—
cheating, lying manipulator.

Courtney Peppernell

I am worth more than the agony I have endured moving on from you. There isn't a single breath left in my lungs that wants to speak your name; there isn't a tear left that wants to cry over your cruelty; there isn't a single thought that wants to be reminded of you. I am reclaiming my life—every breath, tear, and thought; every moment I shed your memory; every step. I grow stronger, every day; I move from your shadow and into the light.

## Out of the Ashes

The trouble with anger
is that, ultimately, it drains
the best of you.

It takes ahold of your heart,
until suddenly it is controlling
every impulse and driving
every beat.

And when you are driven
by anger, the flowers no longer
bloom, the river no longer runs,
even the sun turns cold.

Someday, maybe years from now,
there will be a moment in time
when you will feel regret.

But I will feel nothing.

## Out of the Ashes

I gave you my whole life, and you took it all for granted—
every year we spent together now feels so damn disenchanted.
I thought I knew you well, but you were just an imposter,
thought you had me. Guess what? You fucking lost her.

You lit the match, watched it burn, oh so cool.
Never thought I'd be the one feeling like a fool.

I'm screaming at the top of my lungs, "Why, why, why?!"

Every tear I cried, you never gave a single damn.
Built me up so high, just to break me when you can.
Every promise made, now split open on the floor.
I'm staring at what's left, but I can't find me anymore.

You lit the match, watched it burn, oh so cool.
Never thought I'd be the one feeling like a fool.

I'm done with all your games, the pain you put me through.
This wrath fuels my fire, and I won't be tamed by you.
I'm rising from these ashes, stronger than before.
Your reign is over now; I'm not afraid anymore.

There is nothing baseless about your fury; you have every right to be furious. You're going to want to scream, cry, and sink under your covers until the end of time. Your fury will make you sad, and this sadness will make you want revenge—*If I'm hurt, they should hurt too.* You might feel the urge to throw things, kick things, ball your hands into fists and punch something. And while the fury deserves to be listened to, you don't deserve to be overwhelmed by its consequences. So, I want you to journal—scribble across pages and rip them up if you need to. Watch sad movies that you know will make you cry; let yourself sob and release the pain. Listen to songs that dig up memories, and let them take on new meanings. Walk—walk for more than two miles—because walking clears your mind. It allows you to talk to your fury and move through it with each step. Look at yourself in the mirror and demand that you do everything in your power to heal, because holding your fury accountable will turn it into the strength you need to start again. And remind yourself, every day if you have to: the fury will pass, and you will make it.

## Out of the Ashes

I danced with a scorpion for so long,
And, oh, what a disappointment
they turned out to be.

I heard that the resentment erodes over time,
that eventually I wouldn't feel so bitter.

And, eventually, those things became true.

So, I wrote you a letter, and I burned it,
along with all the things that made me
question love itself.

The final line was this—

"You will never know what it truly means
to love someone, because you are incapable
of loving anyone but yourself."

Courtney Peppernell

You are meant to feel angry
when you have been mistreated.
Anger surges to remind you
of your boundaries
and your own worth—
it is your soul's alarm bells ringing.

Trust this anger; listen to her.

Out of the Ashes

There are some people in this world
who were never meant to escape hell—
I met one once and, blinded by love,
I almost spent forever with them too.
When I say you can survive the devil,
believe me, you will make it through.

There will always be a part of me that remains angry—it does not define me, it does not control my day-to-day, but it's still there, and I don't think it's ever going to go away. I was only ever good to you; I supported you in every dream, every choice, even if some of your choices were questionable. I supported you financially, gave you everything you ever wanted. I took your heart in my hands and I promised not to drop it. And yet, despite the history, seven whole years of it, you cheated. And not in the way someone makes a mistake. Your choices were deliberate, because you continued it, repeatedly. And to me you still spoke of baby names; you still allowed me to get you the things you wanted, still took advantage of me in every way possible. I would have never broken you in that way. I would have never treated you like that. Not once would I have ever destroyed your trust in that way. And yet you treated me that way, without a second thought.

## Out of the Ashes

And you can lie,
you can bend the truth
anyway you like,
but I know what you are,
the kind of person
you turned out to be,
and let me tell you,
you are certainly not
the person for me.

Courtney Peppernell

Know this—
I set myself on fire,
and burned to ash,
just so you wouldn't
get anything more.

I undid myself,
demolished all that I was,
all that I had, all that
I had built, to stop you.

Because I knew,
once you were finally gone,
I would rise again.

# Out of the Ashes

They say misery loves company, and Misery was what I was—so one day, Hate arrived at the doorstep of my heart, and I opened the door wide open.

"Come inside," I said.

Hate paused. "I am responsible for many treacherous things in this world," Hate said to me. "When I live in your heart, I can turn it stone cold."

But I ignored Hate's warning. Instead, I allowed it to take up residence in my heart.

And, oh, how I hated you. I hated you more than anything. I hated the pain you had caused me; I hated the way you violated my soul; I hated your wretched, vile behavior, your entitlement, your lack of empathy.

I wanted you to evaporate, implode, disappear.

Hate lived in my heart—for days and months, and it consumed me.

Until, one day, Hate asked me a question. "Are you not tired?"

"Yes," I replied, for I was so very tired.

I had believed I had no strength left, that Hate had consumed all the light from within me.

So, I said to Hate, "I need you to leave, for there is nothing good that you can do for me."

Hate left.

And I felt lighter.

# The Transformation

## Out of the Ashes

I understand it now—
what we had wasn't real love.
It looked like it,
sounded like it,
but it never existed.

I grieved, I longed for it to return,
I wanted to find a way to go back.

For years, I thought I had found
what I was searching for,
but all it did was bury my heart
beneath waves of sadness.
Then I saw the light—
and I moved toward it.

So it didn't mean that love—the kind
I truly longed for—wasn't out there.
Somewhere, searching for me too.

I mourned, I recovered,
and I flourished.

The life lesson very nearly destroyed me. It was the kind of life lesson in which you dance around the truth, until the universe intervenes. And the universe did intervene. It dealt me an entire deck of cards filled with pain. And I yelled and screamed at the universe, "Where in the script of my life did it say I should have to go through this now? Why did I get handed the worst chapter of my life at a time when I was already hurt and broken on the floor?" It turns out, the universe was not reading any script, because traumatic things can alter a life no matter where it sits on the time line. And while I lost count of all the times when I thought that trauma would end me, the lesson was that it didn't.

Out of the Ashes

I understand: being cheated on hurts. You blame yourself; you rip apart your personality, the way you look, your body, your soul; you question absolutely everything about yourself. And these questions tumble around in your mind— *Why was I not enough? Why did they leave? Why did they choose to hurt me like this?*—like a broken record. And, most days, you will come up empty with answers to these questions. Because, the truth is, it's not you. It's them. One hundred times over, it's them. It doesn't matter how you look at it, upside down, front to back, spin it around again. The common denominator is that they chose themselves first. They chose to give in to their own desires—for whatever reason, it's not important—and act, despite how that choice would impact you. And how you respond is up to you. But consider this: Why give your heart to someone who, in any given moment, thinks more about themselves than they do of you?

—transformation is recognizing your own worth

The shift is never easy. The habit of worrying is deeply rooted. Sometimes the roots go so deep, they will feel impossible to pull. But you must remember that change is a process, not an event. It starts with very small but intentional steps. And the more steps you take, the more you move forward. You are allowed to acknowledge your fears, worries, and anxious thoughts; they are there to help you understand your own boundaries. They are not there to control you—don't give them that kind of power.

The way my trust was broken was deep and earth-shattering. I was the vase, and I had smashed into thousands of tiny pieces. Even if I had begun to haphazardly put myself back together again, the cracks would always be visible. And in the process of the stitching, the gluing, the repairing, I often wondered—if I could be treated so horrendously by the person I had chosen to spend forever with, if they could hurt me on such a level, then surely strangers would do the same or worse.

And then, one day, I met a woman in the park. She was sitting on a bench, reading a book. For whatever reason, I had decided to sit on that bench too. She was using a wildflower as her bookmark. We spoke briefly about how cold the weather had turned, and then we talked about the book she was reading and commented on a dog walking by. And that was all. A brief encounter that I forgot by the next day.

Until I saw her again, on the very same bench. And when I sat down, we spoke of the weather again, about the new book she was reading, and another dog walking by. Over time, I would see the woman regularly at the park. And our conversations changed from the weather and books and dogs to the things that were heavy in my heart. She listened without judgment, she offered advice without condescension, and I began to trust her ability to hold the things that were hurting me. She never tried to fix me; she just accepted me, cracks and all.

And then, one afternoon, she told me her own story of hurt. She showed her own cracks, how she was a vase, too, but she had filled all fractures with wildflowers, now blooming in between the spaces. I saw what I could become. Not someone defined by the things that had hurt them but someone who had grown stronger through it. There was meaning in my healing.

She reminded me that I was not just a vase with cracks; I was a work of art.

You find yourself growing when you understand that, sometimes, in order to build the life you have always wanted, you must first burn some bridges. The people you surround yourself with are meant to bring out the best in you, not the worst. You are meant to feel encouraged, supported, and loved—because these are the ingredients that make someone thrive. You deserve to thrive. What you don't deserve is constant disappointment, constant hurt, constant resentment. When you have boundaries in place, you've communicated these boundaries, and they are ignored repeatedly, every blow has an impact on your heart. You are allowed to burn the bridge so that the things and the people that are toxic to you cannot cross over into the peace you are cultivating.

I wondered how I would ever stop wanting you. The days were easier; I could fill them with things—friends, work, walks, books, anything to distract me. But in the night, I would be filled with memory. If I closed my eyes tight enough, I could still hear your voice, smell you, feel your touch. I held on to that memory. As though it were an old movie, I'd play it again and again, until the film frayed and the picture was grainy, but I just couldn't let it go.

But then, one day, the story changed.

It was born from the strength that had been slowly growing inside me. I began to see you for what you had aways been—the way you had always brought me down. I saw every moment my heart had broken and you'd left it on the floor. And the more I saw, the more the hold you had on me weakened.

And instead, I wondered how I had ever wanted you.

## Out of the Ashes

And everyone kept talking about time
and how it would heal my heart.

I knew all of that to be true because
time and I were old friends.

But it didn't mean the waves didn't crash
down on top of me; it didn't mean the moon
and I didn't cry late into the night;
it didn't mean the trees didn't part
and offer me solace deep in the woods.

I had to spend time going through the grief,
living with it, breathing it, so that eventually
time would untangle me from it.

Self-reflection is difficult; it's bleak and messy. You will see that hill, and you will recognize that it's the hardest hill to climb. Nobody wants to reach deep inside and reevaluate. Because that means change, and change can be frightening. It means speaking of the things that are hurting you, releasing them from the void inside you that you have tried desperately to push down. Suddenly, all those things are floating all around you. It's a heavy conversation; it's exhausting to see all the things that have made you suffer laid out before you. But that is the point—when you lay them all out in front of you, and you see them for what they are, you begin to understand that they are survivable.

Out of the Ashes

You can run from yourself for miles and miles; you can fill your time with people and things to distract yourself; you can push the feelings down deep inside your soul, but it won't matter—the pain will always find you. And it will find you in places you never expect. In the middle of the grocery store, mid-conversation with a friend, while you are waiting in traffic, or in a room full of people. It doesn't pencil you in at a time that suits you; there is no schedule. And it's not your fault. We have been told to get over it, block it out, run away from it. We've been told that to feel things deeply, to feel hurt, to cry, is a weakness. But if you are going to grow, then you must understand pain will always manifest in other ways. The longer you run, the darker it becomes. Facing your pain is not weakness; it's a strength.

There were many things that found me during my process of healing—grief, anxiety, darkness. It was as though I had been a planet, struck by a comet and destroyed. And, suddenly, I was floating among galaxies, searching for the light. As time went by, fragments of who I was and all that I was becoming pulled together, like cosmic dust forming new stars. Every new moment of understanding was a star, and the stars formed constellations. There is an order in the chaos of the universe, a rhythm that even the darkest of black holes cannot disrupt. The gravity was those who loved me, pulling me back to wholeness. Healing was never about returning to what I had been but becoming what I was always meant to be.

## Out of the Ashes

I knew the road would be long, and I knew it would be dark. It was not possible to have been broken in such a way and not expect to have to fight my way out of the misery. I was going to have to go out and search for healing; it would not come to me. Not here, in the ruins of this home. I had to seek it out. But before I left, I asked my old self to leave a light on. For, if I was to search far and wide, I wanted to know that there were still parts of me I could come home to. Surely the brokenness would not completely change me; surely there were still remnants of the person I once was. I did wander far; I wandered so far that I almost disappeared into the shadows. But I could always see that light; I knew where home was. Despite all the suffering, I would find my way back home.

The more distance that grows between the moments it all fell apart and your steps in moving forward, the clearer your perspective becomes. And there will be many little details you once overlooked that you can see now, and they are as clear as crystal waters.

You will see the way that person kept you small, made you feel insignificant, isolated, and controlled. They tried to make you feel worthless.

The more steps you take on your own, the more you see the world in a new light—you see yourself in a new light too. Suddenly you remember who you are, what you are capable of; you understand all the ways in which they tried to extinguish your light.

And I hope you take this clarity with you—for you are worth so much more than they ever gave you credit for; you are so much better off without them.

I think of who I was a year ago
and hardly recognize her.

She has changed and evolved
so much in such a short time.

Because sometimes one year
can feel like an entire lifetime,
but in the grand scheme of life,
it's just a fleeting chapter.

But, oh, what a chapter it was.

I learned so much about who I was,
what I had forgotten, who I was slowly
becoming.

Because we are always becoming
someone different, changed, new.
And that is the beautiful thing
about growth—it is an always.

Courtney Peppernell

And I ask you—
Why do you stay
in the places that break you
when there are places
waiting to love you?

Out of the Ashes

You cannot heal from trauma if you are constantly being re-traumatized. When you open the door to the things or to the people that harm you, and you invite them inside, they make a mess, and you must repeatedly clean that mess up. Imagine your soul as a home that you have worked on your entire life to be a safe space. Every lesson learned, every memory, every high, and every low is a carefully placed piece of furniture, all designed to give you solace. But when you allow these people in, they disrupt your home. They overturn the furniture, they dirty the carpet, they break and shatter things. If you let them stay, they can even destroy your home. They are always leaving you to pick up the pieces. You don't deserve this. You deserve to breathe in your own home. Shut the door on these people; only invite those worthy of making your home the best version it can be.

You tried to tell me that it was all my fault, that we moved at a different frequency—that I was always so sad while you were a shining light. It was true; I was sad. I was sad because I was tired of your selfishness, of your inability to see the needs of anyone but yourself. I was tired of your immaturity, your main-character syndrome, your nonexistent self-awareness. When someone is constantly put down, made to feel worthless, always taken advantage of, over time they begin to believe it. It is like a lily hidden in the shadows, weighed down by darkness, unaware of all the beauty it holds.

It took me so long, but I saw the way things could be. I saw the future I could have, that it didn't have to be filled with dread. That I didn't have to constantly step on eggshells. That somewhere, in some place, there was someone in the world who would love me for who I was and not what I could give them. That I could have the kind of love that was not transactional; it would just be given.

—I could bloom in the light

# Out of the Ashes

Each of us heals in different ways;
this is abundantly true.
But if I may say this—
if you allow those who hurt you
to continue having access to your time,
energy, or generosity, then you are not
holding them accountable for all the ways
they mistreated you.

At the very least, always remember this:
an apology without action is just a word.
Honesty is shown in what you do,
not what you say.

When you live to please others, you are trapped in an exhausting dance of saying yes when you mean no, of sacrificing your own needs to meet the expectations of others, of staying stagnant because you are afraid of moving forward. When you place all your worth into the hands of others, this is not love or acceptance, it is the slow erosion of yourself. You will always be changing to suit others, and you will find yourself so far off the path, you will struggle to find your way back. But there is no such thing as others filling the empty space in your heart. Only you can do that. And you do it by setting boundaries. It won't be easy. The first time you say no, you will feel like you are breaking all the rules. But with every no comes a sense of purpose, for you are reclaiming pieces of yourself that have been long lost. You will learn that saying no to others is saying yes to yourself—your needs, wants, desires, well-being. This is how you grow, by understanding that your value is not in how much you can give to others but in how much you honor your own needs.

It's difficult to look inward. You'll delay and delay because you are afraid of the things you'll find when you unpack it all. It's like finding an abandoned suitcase; if you rummage through all of its contents, will you find a cute vintage sweater, or will you find an old worn-out pair of shoes. In actuality, you will find both. Because that is life. When you unpack the suitcase of your life, you are going to find things that uplift you and things that break you. It is a constant flow. But the courage is in the unpacking, the reevaluating, the hope that things will get better the more you choose to work on yourself.

Courtney Peppernell

By honoring your hurt,
a new door appears,
and through that door
is your ability to transform.

Too often, we bury our hurt,
we push it away,
pretend it does not exist.

And so the door to something
more for ourselves never appears.

When you stop resisting and
start listening to your pain,
you are giving yourself permission
to open the door.

There is nothing shameful about changing your mind or changing course. You don't have to know everything in your twenties, thirties, forties, or beyond. In truth, you are never going to know everything there ever is, and that is okay. Life could be predictably predictable for years and years, and then suddenly something erupts, sending you spinning off into a completely new direction. The change will have you tumbling before you can walk again, but you will survive.

Courtney Peppernell

There is no loud explosion
in transformation.

It begins slowly, small,
an unseen seed planted deep
in the soil of who you are.

You think nothing is happening;
you believe the days go by
one after the other in the same way
they always have—
uneventful and stagnant.

But the roots of you are quietly
spreading, grasping for strength
beneath the surface.

And then, one day, it seems
to happen out of the blue:
you bloom.

You unfurl in the morning light,
dewy, glowing, and beautiful.

The world sees only a flower,
not the darkness and effort
it grew through.

But you'll know.
You'll know.

## Out of the Ashes

You will spend so much time trying
to piece yourself back together again,
hoping to re-create what once was.

But the pieces don't need to fit anymore;
you are no longer the same shape.

—you will outgrow yourself

Courtney Peppernell

And I know you
will feel like giving up,
throwing it all away.
For if there is only grief,
then where do you find
the light in every day?

And in the harsher months,
when life seems broken
all the way through,
remember, there is courage
buried deep within you.

To find it will take some nerve—
for sorrow may surround you,
and tears may often fall,
but they are only reminders
of the resilience in us all.

Know that, even through pain,
your hope can still rise,
even amid the darkness,
there are stars in the night skies.

## Out of the Ashes

You won't look back on your life
wishing you had made yourself smaller.

But you might wish
you had taken up the space
you worked so hard to build.

Beyond your fears,
beyond the noise of doubt,
lives the version of you
who fills her own cup,
who stands up for what she deserves,
who demands respect without apology.

Pull back the curtain—set her free.

Life is not a straight line but a series of twists and turns that shapes you in a way that you may not immediately recognize. With every change and every unexpected detour, your soul learns. You will be amazed at just how much you can grow. How different you will become as the years move by. Sometimes, you'll look back at yourself, who you used to be, and it'll be like night and day. Doors will close, chapters will end, jars will be empty, but equally so, too, will doors open, new chapters begin, and jars be filled once more.

## Out of the Ashes

Everything I had ever been felt like it was ending everywhere. And I had to sit with this ending. I had faith the new beginning would come for me. I didn't know when or how, but I knew it would arrive. And while I waited, I asked myself, *Are you dreaming enough? Do you still believe in stars? Do you still fold napkins in half and write on either side? Do you go for long walks, search for the birds in the trees? Do you have two scoops of ice cream from your favorite creamery, and midday naps on Sunday afternoons? Are you still you, even after everything came crashing down?* There is room for the past while you make way for the future. You can carry parts with you into new beginnings.

Courtney Peppernell

And then you meet someone one day,
and they take the time to understand
how you need to be loved.

You meet someone who doesn't punish
you for the past, who learns of the things
that have happened to you and never
judges you for the baggage you carry.

You meet someone who would rather
be the person who stays.

Out of the Ashes

There is a balcony somewhere; it faces the sun in the late afternoon. It overlooks the tallest oak trees; you can see the hummingbirds as their wings beat against the sky, a song whispering through the breeze. You and I are here, your arm is draped across my lap, we are sipping tea and honey. You are reminding me of plans we made the other week, and I am nodding; I could never forget all the things we want to do together. Somewhere, I am sitting here with you, I've finally found you, and you've found me.

—I look for you in the stars

I surprised myself in how I learned to trust again. Believe me, it took work. I had to separate the way I had been hurt in the past from my fear that it would happen again. I had to give all the same chances to someone new that I had given to the person who broke me entirely. But I learned that there are still good people in the world, and just because someone hurts you doesn't mean that everyone will. There are still people in the world who will be kind to you, even if kindness had not been shown to you previously. There are still good people who will treat you with respect and genuine care and who will love you unconditionally; they are out there.

## Out of the Ashes

The ache of today is here,
but there is always tomorrow,
and it will hurt a little less.

You cannot grow
without compromise—
you must feel the ache,
hear it deep in your soul,
so that, eventually, it may pass.

Even if you cannot change
where you have been,
or how things are now,
you can always change the way
you encourage yourself to persist.

The new season is coming—fall to winter, winter to spring, spring to summer, summer to fall, and all over again—and maybe this season will bring joy or change or fear or turmoil. But no matter what it brings, you'll move through each week. The crisp chill of fall, the stillness of winter, the hopeful bloom of spring, the warmth of summer, and there are lessons in each. And maybe you will feel overwhelmed or uncertain when the leaves fall and world turns cold, but the quiet is a time for reflection, to recharge before you will bloom afresh. Every season will mold you into something more. So, keep your feet steady, grounded in every moment. Let your heart remain open to love, connection, and new experiences. Declutter your mind of doubt and fear so that you can remain clear and in control. It doesn't matter what the season brings, because it's all impermanent, and the next season is right around the corner.

# Out of the Ashes

I notice when you don't laugh,
and it breaks my soul.

To watch you as you unfold,
and bare it all to the universe,
all the while hoping you are
not too much,
how can I convey to you all
that has happened,
has happened as it should?

And I know it feels like people
just look right through you—
why else would you go so far
into your own head?
Is anyone even listening?

I hope somehow you know your worth,
even if it is buried deep down inside,
having to crawl its way to the surface.

Courtney Peppernell

It was lovely, the way I saw the color again
in every flower, every painting, every sunset,
the way it erupted from the moment we met.

And, undoubtedly, I was changed by you,
like I knew your soul from the first glance.
Even if I never have the right words to explain,
I knew, in that moment, I had a second chance.

Out of the Ashes

Things are temporary—and while that is a difficult truth for the things we love, like long summers at the beach, a good book, or moments that bring us joy, it is also true for the things that hurt us, like a broken heart, a painful loss, a missed opportunity. Just as the leaves change, so do our circumstances. It is a lesson that holds weight, the idea that moments are so fleeting. If you let yourself, you will find a way to cherish the beautiful moments spectacularly. Even the ordinary moments become something special, something to live for. All you can do is embrace it, this temporary nature of everything; you hold on to hope in every storm and savor the light in every new day. Because the promise is this—all heartache eventually leaves.

Courtney Peppernell

These boundaries that I have created
are not walls to keep people out
but rather guides to protect my heart.

I give more now than I ever have,
because of them.

Because it comes from a place
of fullness and not depletion.

It takes so much work to arrive at a place where you can look at yourself and think, *I love who you are.* Of course, there is always room for improvement—you can always improve your communication, understand boundary setting, find ways to be more compassionate and kinder to those around you. But, ultimately, when you arrive at a place where you accept all your little quirks and habits and the way you are, there is something in the way you hold yourself that shines a little brighter. Which is why there is no place in your life for people undermining you or belittling you. It is the very thing that can undo all the work you have put into yourself. Don't give anyone the opportunity to do that.

May you find what you are looking for one day—I hope it's joy, in whatever form it may take: a house along the coast, the tiny patter of feet running down the hall, playing fetch in the yard with your dog and a ball. Maybe it's singing on the grandest of stages or writing books and stories that are timeless for the ages. Maybe it's in the way you have come back from the brink, or your courage to say no to a drink. In any way, shape, or form, no matter what happiness looks like for you, I hope you find it, in the same way the birds always find the skies. And just in case you haven't heard it lately, my greatest wish is for you to rise.

Out of the Ashes

Plan for things, for what you want, and what you hope to achieve. Plan for the life you want, the dreams you have, and the love you need. Plan it all out, and have courage if some plans don't work out. Because the simple truth is, life rarely goes to plan. You are always going to have more growing to do, you are always going to need to heal from something or someone, you are always going to have habits to break and lessons to uncover and more acceptance to deliver. But every now and then, pause to see how far you have come. Because you have come far. From where you were, to where you are, there are miles in between. And you tracked every mile, and you built your strength, and you earned every single moment. Be proud of yourself, okay?

The worst part of trying to heal and start over was the constant second-guessing. What was normal—a bad day, a miscommunication, an error in judgment—was compounded by the fact that anytime I made a mistake, I believed I was the worst person in the world. Because this is what I had been taught. That I was never allowed to make mistakes, that everything was always my fault, that I was too emotional and took everything too seriously. When you have lived with that, then the normal mistakes any human being is allowed to make suddenly make you feel like everything in the entire universe is wrong with you. It became this cycle of relentless criticism, wherein even the tiniest misstep felt like a catastrophic failure. I would replay conversations repeatedly, convinced I had said something wrong. But as I unraveled more threads, I realized that the darkened voice was not coming from my soul but that rather it had been infiltrated by a master manipulator. The only way I was able to find hope in the morning was by accepting my own humanity—we are not lesser because someone else has deceived us. When we understand that we have capacity for growth, we emerge on the other side with the faith that our soul can be both tender and strong.

Out of the Ashes

In late September, when the air was crisp and the asters were in full bloom, Forgiveness met me on my favorite trail. We walked together, side by side, along a riverbank, the trees whispering in the breeze. "I am not willing to forgive them," I said to Forgiveness, "not for the way they wronged me; they do not deserve it." "They do not," Forgiveness agreed gently, "but you do."

And as we walked, I realized how heavy each step was—life shouldn't feel like you are bound by chains. I let my anger and resentment wash away in the current of the river. But I made the choice; it was my decision, on my own terms. There was no need to forgive the person who had betrayed me; they were not worthy. But I was. Their actions no longer needed to chain me.

I define the way I moved forward, not them.

Courtney Peppernell

The heart can hold
many things at once—
you can be in the deepest
pockets of sorrow
and still know joy.

When I was learning to give myself love, I knew I needed to pull myself up every mountain. I needed to continue moving, continue growing, continue healing so that I would emerge into the daylight. I have been burned so many times. Set alight so that all that remained was ash. But I recovered. When it storms, because it will always storm, the storms are not as loud. There are words I can say, and I choose to say them now. I am not afraid to do things; I do not let people walk all over me. When you spend so long questioning yourself, the moment you begin to trust yourself is a truly remarkable feeling.

My healing went back and forth. There were days when I could see how far I had come, and then there were days when it felt like I had taken ten steps backward. But all in all, life is such a curious thing. One moment, my life was falling apart, and I could not imagine a day when everything would be fine again. But time moved forward, and the clocks continued ticking, and the world moved on, and so did I. Days turned into weeks and weeks into months, and suddenly a year had passed, and I was happier than I had ever been. I had not forgotten the ache, or the nights when my soul felt shattered into oblivion, but the point was that I could think about it from time to time and it didn't hurt like it used to. It will always be one of life's greatest riddles, how in the moments of suffering we cannot see our courage or resilience, but it's there, it's always there, and time steps in to remind us.

Out of the Ashes

Remember all the times
when you were afraid,
but you carried on anyway?

It is always possible to start over.

You can choose differently,
you can take chances, risks,
become a better version
of the person you want to be.

I wrote a letter to myself, and I told her that I was sorry. I was sorry for taking so long to love her. I was sorry for all the times I had discarded her worth, belittled her mind, and failed to see her beauty. I was sorry for all the moments when I had let fear control us, all the days when I had silenced her voice, and all the long nights when I had questioned her very existence. I promised her things were going to change, that we were emerging as someone new—someone who respected our time, our heart, our right to be treated well. I told her that, for every time the journey shifted, I would not run or hide, that I was braver now, that I believed in her more. I gave her permission to forgive herself, to heal and to move forward. I encouraged her to open her heart again, because there was no reason to keep it closed. I breathed relief as I told her that, against everything we had ever thought to be true, I'd finally learned I was enough.

Out of the Ashes

Life is meant to scare you. It is not human to avoid anxiety, fear, stress, and worry. There is no need to pretend as though life is not some constant game of tug-of-war. When you stop pretending that you have a handle on everything, the real beauty reveals itself. It is in the way you listen to your heart and to your happiness as equally as you listen to and acknowledge your worst fears and the things that hurt you. And when the day clears for the first time in a long time, and the worry and fear leaves, you will remember what it feels like to breathe.

One day, she came to me,
and she said, "I've felt so lost,
I didn't know which way
was north.

"But today, something arrived,
a shift in who I am, and I knew
what choices to make and
which way to go."

And I loved her a little more
in that moment,
because to see her find herself again
was as beautiful as watching the sun
rise again and splash color
all over the world after a storm.

## Out of the Ashes

"I feel like I am changing."

"That's because you are," said the moon.
"Sometimes you have to let go of who you were
to become who you were meant to be."

"I still feel the ache in my chest sometimes."

"Healing always takes time," said the sun.
"You must remember, every scar tells a story
of your survival."

"I have made so many mistakes."

"Everyone makes mistakes," said the universe.
"But you are still loved more than life."

The entire sky was stretched out before you, and you wondered where the light had gone, for it had been so long since you had seen it. And even in the depths of such darkness, you must remember, there is always someone who will call you right when you need them to. There is always someone thinking about you, waiting to see you again. There is always someone who stays up late for you. Somewhere along the road, you have forgotten how loved you are. You've been told you belong in the shadows, that anything you do isn't worthy of love or pride or recognition. You've banished your heart to the dark lands. And it will only ever stay bitter there.

Do you not see the way the sky stares back at you, how the moon holds space for you, the way the world stops just to see you move by? Someday, you will open the windows and the doors and call your heart back home. And you'll see that the light had always been left on for you, and you'll breathe deeper than you have in years.

## Out of the Ashes

You know your heart best;
it's learning to trust yourself again—
that is the thing that takes time.

Courtney Peppernell

I truly thought the end
was where I'd always stay.
But every night will fade
and make way for a new day.
With every sunrise,
a promise to start again—
and this time,
in the sky will be my name.

# Out of the Ashes

Here is what I love about new beginnings—they are the dawn after a long night, the first breath of fresh air after a storm. They are the first brushstroke on a blank canvas; they are the turning of a page, the start of a new chapter. They whisper to us the promise that anything is possible, that if we let the past fall away, then our dreams can take root and grow. They are the heart of every journey, always defining and redefining everything we do.

—every end is a new beginning in disguise

Sitting in the dust taught me about timing. I could not rise again until I had done the work. But also, to rise was to accept that there would be many more times when I would fall and have to pull myself back up again. Life isn't about having all the answers; it's about living in every moment, learning the lessons handed to me. I needed to trust the journey I had been placed on, trust that it was meant for me. Changing course was not the end of my life, even though it had felt like it was; instead, it was the beginning of the life I was always meant to have. I am always going to be a work in progress. I am not afraid of that anymore.

It's a beautiful thing.

Out of the Ashes

It is never too late. You are allowed to start over. You can reinvent yourself one hundred times in one hundred different ways; it doesn't matter. What matters is your courage to take every day as it comes and to have the desire to change and willingness to grow. The determination is buried deep inside you; you only need to light the fire within and find the things that truly fulfill you. You are not just your name, or an age, or numbers on a scale. You are not the mistakes you have made, or the regrets you carry, or the decisions you wish to change. Rather, you are the smile you have when you see something or someone you love. You are your favorite day of the week; you are the mountains you have climbed, the roads you have traveled, the light in your eyes when you achieve hard things, the colors when you dream. You are all the lessons you have learned.

Courtney Peppernell

We were once a poem
I thought would last
forever,
but endings
can be beginnings too.
It's my time now;
I'm going to write
myself whole again.

Out of the Ashes

I lived my life cloaked in doubt. I did not think my opinion held any worth. So, it would always leave me on a tipping scale—*Do I stay or do I go? Do I let go or do I hold on?*—and because of this, it made me reclusive instead of assertive. I chose to hide instead of stand out; I always felt afraid instead of brave. Until, suddenly, I was an apparition of myself, like at any moment I could fade into the background and disappear. And it did not matter how many times I tried to look the other way; I couldn't escape that feeling of never being good enough. The more I lived, the more I struggled, and the cloak became heavier and heavier. Until the day arrived when I looked at myself in one hundred different ways, all different outcomes, and I continued arriving in the same place—*If I deny my worth, I deny my life.* There was only one thing to do. I left the cloak at the door, and I went back out into the world. I demanded respect, I embraced my truth, and I faced my fears. And it led me to a place where doubt no longer ruled my life.

Courtney Peppernell

A year ago, I looked out at barren trees
in the forest along my fence line;
I felt as though they were me.

I was dead inside.

Robbed of all the fruit and sweetness
by an unforgiving winter.

But the trees were not dead.

The leaves regrew and the birds returned.

And I watched the birds as they came and went
and imagined hope as wings;
without them, you cannot fly.

Out of the Ashes

Let me tell you—I grew tired of hearing the words "be the bigger person." As though I needed to accept when others had wronged me, treated me poorly, or behaved unfairly. As though it was me who had to take the high road when someone else had been the one to run a steamroller right through my path. As though I just had to settle for the way I had been used, spat out, and taken advantage of. And yes, retaliation and revenge never truly make us feel any better—all the way down in the depths of our core—but being the bigger person is not permission for others to walk all over you. You don't have to tolerate insincere apologies or continuously spend your valuable time on people who only ever exhaust you. You don't need to be in the business of showing up for those who do not show up for you. Being the bigger person means choosing maturity, kindness, and integrity for yourself, and protecting your space.

Your life has been moving; it's been moving all along, and it's going by quickly. One day, you are fifteen and you're wondering if you will ever belong. Then you're twentysomething and you've convinced yourself you can change the world. Then you're thirtysomething and you know better. And you suddenly wake up one morning and you wonder where all the time has gone—*How did it go by so quickly?* And that's just it, isn't it? You blink and you're already at the finish line. So, all those moments in between, feel them all. From every heartache to every happiness, one does not exist without the other. You do not live until everything around you collapses and you emerge again every once in a while.

Out of the Ashes

You will live with fear and doubt your whole life; they are roommates who never leave. But you can live with them. You just have to very pointedly tell them to go to hell every once in a while. You won't win every argument; you aren't supposed to. You are meant to be wrong every now and then. It teaches you humility; it teaches you to accept that other people have different opinions. Comparison will keep you up at night when it doesn't have to. Stop comparing yourself with other people; you are not living their journey, and they are not living yours. A fireman puts out fires, a chef cooks, a football player plays football—if you want to be something, then do it. Wash your sheets, clean the dishes, put out the garbage, walk your dog. If you have children, be there for them; they are only children once. Breathe. Breathe some more. Give, but don't waste your generosity on those who don't deserve it. Yes, time does make you grow; it also heals. But neither means you have to forget.

There have been many versions of myself, for I am always
    reinventing—
we learn, and then we evolve, and then we learn
    some more.

One night, the old me appeared in a dream;
she came to me in the space between the sky and the sea.
I said to her, "Just look how far you have come,"
and she replied, "I was unsure back then. I was timid
    and afraid;
I could not see my worth."

She said, "Thank you for standing up for us, for
    letting us escape
and become stronger. For all the times when we were
    battered and torn
to shreds, thank you for finally saying 'No more.'"

And I said quietly but more sure than ever—"My friend, I
did it for you."

## Out of the Ashes

Sometimes there is no reason for grief—
it just hits you out of nowhere.
And you'll be somewhere, deep in a hole,
unable to see all the most wonderful things
about you and all the things you could be.
You know what makes me sad the most?
You not knowing your own worth.

Courtney Peppernell

"I don't know what I am doing!"
you will scream into an endless void.

And if you listen,
you'll hear the void scream back—
"Neither do I!"

Because uncertainty will always exist.

It doesn't matter where you have been,
or where you are headed, the more emphasis
you place on having everything worked out,
the more you will disappoint yourself.

Instead, you can measure yourself by what
you do know—honeybees are remarkable,
fresh air should be breathed in deeply,
salt water is good for the soul, those who
truly love you are those who are there
through it all.

Out of the Ashes

There was always that feeling that I knew something just wasn't quite right. But I ignored it. I let the fear take over; I let the second-guessing stand in the way of my own intuition. And it took me forever to reason with my heart, because my heart held on to hope for so long. Hope that things would change, hope that we were destined for more, hope that everything would be okay so long as I was patient. But it didn't matter how patient I was, how much I hoped, how much I waited; I was always going to have the same feeling. Because when your soul knows, it does not let it go. It holds on until your heart catches up. When you have that feeling, those deep-seated roots of something feeling wrong, lean into them; it is your soul telling you something is not right for you.

Courtney Peppernell

You and I are sitting somewhere with a beautiful view, but you don't count the clouds in the sky or notice the birds flying by. You don't see the way the lake changes color depending on the time of day; you aren't listening to the trees whisper or anything I have to say—but you are worried, for the week and years ahead, for all the things that could go wrong, and all the things to dread. You let your coffee go cold, never having taken a sip, this is what they mean when you aren't present in the now; you just miss all of it.

## Out of the Ashes

She watched me as I healed. She was there, every step of the way. It wasn't intentional, the way we met; we somehow collided. I had been hurt, reduced to a colorless shell of a person. But I was surviving. I was finding ways to heal, to patch and stitch up my heart. And at first, I thought, *Perhaps it is too soon. Perhaps I should retreat into the cave. Am I really ready?* The truth is, you're never ready. Not when you have been hurt so badly. The truth is you have to take the leap anyway. So, I did. And she was as patient as she was kind; she was as understanding as she was supportive. And I arrived at a place where I could not imagine a world in which I was never stepping in time with her—because that is the beautiful thing about healing: you can do it, even while you're falling in love.

You can know your worth, you can find it, you can harness it, and you can wield it. But it is useless unless you remind yourself of it. Because you are going to have many moments when you feel like absolutely nothing. When the thoughts and opinions of others outweigh the opinion you have of yourself. You are going to stand there, fear coursing through your veins, wondering if standing your ground is going to shake the foundations of the relationships you have with others. And that is the point—relationships built on shaky ground, on which people manipulate and walk all over you, are not healthy relationships.

Out of the Ashes

You know you have options. You don't need to settle because someone else tells you to. If you let go of the idea that your life is going to go in a certain way, and if you are open to the tides changing, the sky looking different every day, and the way a current can shift and change, then the new paths won't feel as though you have been completely destroyed; instead, they will feel exciting, like you have been given another chance.

Courtney Peppernell

If there is ever a day when
you do not feel loved,
know that I love you.

If there is ever a time when
you feel scared and hurt,
know that I am right here.

In all the moments
you feel lost and alone,
remember that my heart
is your heart;
it is always beating for you.

I am on your side,
wishing you the very best,
to see it all through.

Because this is the basis
of love—
I am always here for you.

Out of the Ashes

Trust that there is someone out there looking for you, hoping to find you. There is someone, somewhere, dreaming of you, of the love you hold in your heart; they are waiting, hoping, searching for everything that you are. They wonder about the day your paths will cross, when the stars will align and they will finally meet the person they've wished for. Believe in the power of connection, that love has a way of finding its way, even when you don't expect it. In the meantime, focus on yourself, build your boundaries, work on that self-confidence. The kind of love you deserve is out there.

Courtney Peppernell

There are some people
you can just look at and know—
you're going to change my life.

And maybe it's for better or worse,
but they'll change you.

Yet it's you who decides
what to do with the change.

Should tomorrow never arrive, I wanted to leave you with some thoughts—you'll live the hardest years of your life, and you'll get to the end and wonder how you made it, but the point is, you did. Every now and then, you'll hold in tears, an ache, try to push it down—don't. Release the tears; crying is good for you. The same for laughter. Laugh every chance you get; feel it deep down in the pit of your belly. We are so often consumed with the motions of life, we fail to see the things around us. Stop and look up every now and then, the way the stars glint against a night sky. See the new wildflowers that have come to bloom. Smell fresh bread as it's baked and wafting down the street. Touch the sand with your toes; dig them all the way in. Listen to the call of birds and the hum of an old steam train. Look at the way a fresh coat of paint makes all the difference and how much people love their dogs. Feel everything. Even the things you are afraid of. Respect yourself and those around you. Say the words "I love you" often. Go home every once in a while and hug the people who love you. We don't have very long in the whole scheme of things; make it count.

Courtney Peppernell

You thought
I'd stay down—
But, instead, I rise.

Each and every time.

A phoenix,
born from ash,
I am made of fire;
now just watch me
as I burn brighter.

Out of the Ashes

That was the thing—
I had known my worth.
I knew it cover to cover.

But then I met you and,
over time, you erased every line
of every chapter of every page,
until, suddenly, the story
of my worth had all but disappeared.

This is what it meant to survive you.

I had to dig up my worth
and rewrite my story.

I sat down with my heart one day, and I told her that, for all the ache she had experienced, there would be so many more things that brought her joy. I told her that strength will always come and go and that every year will not be the same. It will change day by day and season by season, but that she deserved to be loved in every beat.

I sat down with my mind, and I told her that, for every time she questioned the road, to stay on it and stay focused. I told her she would find every reason under the sun not to continue forward, but that was just fear talking. I told her she would argue with herself, about her capability and her strength, but even if winter feels endless, spring always returns.

I sat down with my soul, and I told her that she was worthy. That the battle scars she wore were not indicators of the life she would lead. I told her that her wholeness was not dependent on other people but rather on all the ways she respected the things she needed.

I gathered my heart, mind, and soul, and I told them, "This life we live will feel like a thousand years, but really, it goes by in a blink—so give everything you have."

## Out of the Ashes

So, you have faced an unimaginable betrayal,
shaking the foundations of all that you knew,
threatening to destroy your soul without fail,
shattering all the things you believed were true.

Yes, indeed, all that you were came to an end;
your days were thrown into the dark and quiet
as you tried to navigate where hope descends—
sometimes fueled by wrath and a desire to riot.

But as sure as all the lessons were finally learned,
so, too, was your ability to recover your spark.
And through every tear and triumph earned,
you saw light in the very depths of your heart.

And that spark grew, slowly, to a flame so great,
a reminder that your courage was not up for debate.
For even though the betrayal destroyed your trust,
your soul persisted through all the ache and dust.

Even in all the ways you were discarded and broken,
you rose to new heights and reached for the sky;
all the while, your heart and soul remained open,
finding resilience in that your spark would never die.

Life will always be changing; it is meant to evolve.
But no matter how often it tumbles and crashes,
remember your strength and your own resolve—
just know in your heart, you will rise from the ashes.

# *Thank you for reading this book*

I hope you enjoyed reading it as much as I enjoyed writing it. You can stay up to date with all my latest news and projects via my website, www.peppernell.com.

Feel free to write to me via courtney@pepperbooks.org.

*Pillow Thoughts app now available on iOS and Android stores, worldwide and on all devices—download yours today for your daily poetry!*

Discover more books in the series.
Available online and in all good bookstores!

**WATERING THE SOUL**

**THE WAY BACK HOME**

**TIME WILL TELL**

**A MONTH OF SUNDAYS**

*Out of the Ashes* copyright © 2025 by Courtney Peppernell. All rights reserved. Printed in the United States of America. No part of this book may be used or reproduced in any manner whatsoever without written permission, except in the case of reprints in the context of reviews.

The authorised representative in the EEA is Simon and Schuster Netherlands BV, Herculesplein 96 3584 AA Utrecht, Netherlands. (info@simonandschuster.nl)

Andrews McMeel Publishing
a division of Andrews McMeel Universal
1130 Walnut Street, Kansas City, Missouri 64106

www.andrewsmcmeel.com

25 26 27 28 29 VEP 10 9 8 7 6 5 4 3 2 1

ISBN: 979-8-8816-0186-7

Library of Congress Control Number: 2025934752

Editors: Patty Rice and Danys Mares
Art Director: Diane Marsh
Production Editor: Elizabeth A. Garcia
Production Manager: Julie Skalla

ATTENTION: SCHOOLS AND BUSINESSES
Andrews McMeel books are available at quantity discounts with bulk purchase for educational, business, or sales promotional use. For information, please email the Andrews McMeel Publishing Special Sales Department: sales@andrewsmcmeel.com.